Email Marketing Guru

Table Of Contents

Foreword

Using the electronic mailing system otherwise known as the email is one way of sending a commercial message to a target group audience. This is done for the purpose of getting the desired attention for the business through internet marketing platforms. You get all the help and info you need here.

Email Marketing Mogul
Tips For Email Campaigns That Really Work

Chapter 1:

Email Marketing Basics For Internet Marketing

Synopsis

Emails can function as various different avenues to get the attention of the intended party. Some of these functions may include sending ads, requesting business participation, soliciting sales or donations and may other internet related business propositions.

The Basics

This form of communication is ideally meant to build some level of trust, loyalty and brand awareness. The email marketing exercise can be done through a cold list or form a current customer database thus the range of the target audience can be almost infinite.

This internet marketing through the email platform is also meant to create other idea scenarios.

These may include the sending of email messages with the specific intention of facilitating the avenue of building a relationship between the merchant with its available customer base while at the same time tapping into the previous and possible future customer bases.

This is done primarily to foster better ties so that these emails can eventually function as a way to acquire new customers or convince existing customers to make an immediate purchase.

Some may even use the email tool to send messages to their customers regarding beneficial and supportive things available at other companies or sites for purchase which they perceive to be helpful to the customer.

There are several types of email styles that can be used for the purpose of conducting internet marketing exercises, such as email newsletters, transactional emails; direct emails and all these have

their own individual advantages. Also using the emails in this fashion
will be comparatively a cheaper form of advertising for the business.

Chapter 2:

Synopsis

The popular saying that time is money is very true more so in today's very pressed for time world. There does not seem to be enough time for anything and more often than not emails get deleted even before they are opened because people simply do not have the time to spare with what they perceive to be a waste of theirs.

To The Point

Therefore is one is intending to use the email campaign as an effective tool for internet marketing some very important rules or recommendations should be very carefully considered.

The primary points that often cause an email to be disregarded often lies in the actual design and presentation of the said email. In order to gain the attention of the potential viewer the email presentation has only a very small fraction of time to grab the individual's attention.

If this is not done almost immediately, then the opportunity is definitely lost and thus the email discarded.

Next if this attention grabbing point has been successfully addressed then there needs to be some thought given to the relevance of the email content.

If the target audience deems the material irrelevant to them again the possibility of discarding the email is high indeed. Therefore it is important to consider if the material is not only relevant but as informative as possible without seeming too technical or boring to ensure the receiving party is happy to be included in the list of the particular email campaign exercise.

Also because time is money there should be some consideration given to ensure the content is designed to be short and to the point.

Without being too pushy in the sales pitch the product must be featured and all positive points made within the shortest possible amount of words. Including some eye catching visual effects might help too.

Chapter 3:
Don't Be So Formal, Write With Personality

Synopsis

There are many ways to design email content to act as the first presentation material the potential customer is going to be viewing. However perhaps the most important point to keep in mind is to consider and ensure the content is designed according to the receiving party's perception of what is acceptable and impressive and what is not.

Show Yourself

There is a fine line between being too formal and being too casual, thus careful consideration should be given to the intention of the email, the product being touted and the person receiving it.

Loosely meaning that if the recipient is to be addressed in his or her capacity as a member of a company and representing its interest then the email may be expected to take on a more formal tone but if the email is meant to tweak an individual's interest on a more personal basis then perhaps the tone should be changed accordingly to a less formal one.

However having said this, it would also not really serve any purpose to keep the tone of the email so formal that it becomes almost superficial and without any personal connecting connotations.

Using the personal touch as a measurable bench mark and trying to design the mail as closely as if the individual was making a presentation in person would give the email a more exciting an approachable tone.

This will also help the recipient to connect to the general content, more so if it is designed in an interactive way. The personality of the sender should ideally be felt and the email should also create a sense of comfort and trust between the two parties.

Establishing a slightly more personal platform to work on through the initial email will adequately provide for any future exchanges.

- 13 -

Chapter 4:

Using Teasers And Your Links

Synopsis

The attention grabbing window is comparatively very small for most people therefore it is important to optimize any attention directed to the email especially if it is only for a second. Using tools like teasers and links if well designed will help to optimize the chances of getting and retaining the attention of the viewer.

Getting Attention

Some points to consider when designing teasers may include the following:

- Choosing the best medium is necessary for the success of the email design. The press medium may be chosen for it small enticing ads which usually appears on several pages leading up to the main page. Then there are the online banners and flashes which could be provocative in nature which would entice the viewer to explore further.

- Design the teaser to be directed at the needs of the recipient. If the product can reflect this need than the chances of perking the recipient's interest is even better. Keep the direct personal approach foremost in the design work, toward giving the perception that the recipient is the only and important element in the equation.

- Teasers should also be designed to attract the recipient curiosity. Curiosity always makes an individual pose questions that creates the initial exchange of ideas phase. This exchange once established is a step in the right direction and should be capitalized upon.

- Another beneficial element to include is the use of links. The links should further enhance the content matter as it will assist in introducing other related sites to the recipient. These links if featured from a reputable website can increase the chances of being picked up by search engines which in turn makes the contents seem more relevant and popular. This popularity angle will further perk the interest of the recipient.

- Understanding the profile of the recipient will lead to better usage of appropriate links whereby the potential of the email marketing style is enhanced.

Chapter 5:
Using The Best Frequency For Marketing Mail

Synopsis

Being bombarded with emails especially if they are of the unwanted kind can not only be a nuisance but can also be quite annoying especially if time is wasted deleting them. This unnecessary waste of resources should not be evident in the email exercise of the individual campaign as it would eventually affect its relevance.

The Timing

Therefore it is very important to decide the appropriate frequency that should be applied to suit each individual targeted through the email campaign.

Overexposure is just as detrimental to any email campaign as underexposure is because this will eventually contribute to the loss of potential sales and customer interests.

Through overexposure the intended customer will feel overwhelmed with the emails sent or they may even feel they are being spammed.

With the underexposure there is the possibility of losing out on opportunities and sales which may have otherwise been successfully made because the recipient received insufficient emails and reminders.

Generally an assessment should be made on the impact the email marketing campaign is making on the customer activity and perception.

If the frequency rate is being launched at a rather high pace then the obvious results would be for the recipient to disengage themselves from receiving the emails.

This can be done by using the aggregate open and click rates that are recorded by most email broadcasting systems. Another way to make an assessment is to look at the average number of emails received in return by the subscribers over a set period of time.

This set period could be anything from one week to one year or anything to be perceived to be a suitable time gauge for the campaign.

By gathering information and studying the data from this exercise, the sender will be able to make a more informed decision on the frequency suitable for each campaign.

Chapter 6:

Author Great Headlines To Keep Your E-mail Out Of The Trash

Synopsis

The headline of an email is often the only window the sender has to capture and retain the attention of the target audience. The impression made based on the headline posted will be instrumental in ensuring the viewer continues to show interest in the posting. Therefore it is very important to acquire the relevant skill to ensure the best choices are made in relation to the headlines.

Capture Attention

The following are some suggestions and considerations:

- The secret of ......this is a good headline because most people like the idea of being able to crack a good secret. Fancying themselves to be part of the privileged few is enough to draw the attention of most individuals.

- A quick and easy......also another attention grabber because it implies the least amount of work or effort needed to get optimum results. This definitely tunes into the average individual who looks for ways to exercise the least amounts of efforts to get things done.

- Now you can............. Is attention grabbing because it creates the perception of power in the individual's hands thus making the prospect of being in total control worth exploring. Besides this it also implies the encouragement and probability of being able to adequately provide solutions to problems.

- Being an expert of............people are often attracted to this type of headline as they would like to explore anything that implies it can provide the platform for fine tuning skills to be the best. Everyone wants to be an authority in their chosen area.

- How to..........are also equally popular attention grabbing headlines and there are always an incredible amount of tips and clues on getting things done easily and seemingly painlessly.

- (Number) ways to.... Is purported to be the most popular by far probably because of its more concise form of providing information and tips to the subject at hand.

Chapter 7:

Incorporate Some Great Free Training

Synopsis

The idea of anything free is a potential attractive attention attracting point. This is further enhanced when it promises a certain amount of skill acquiring possibilities. In order to encourage the visitor to explore further it would be beneficial to provide some type of free training session.

Freebies

The free training can also act as an incentive that can be acquired only upon committing in some way to what is being advertised.

Therefore if the visitor was interested in the training session advertised as free, then making the commitment required would pose little or no problem at all.

The free training tool can go a long way to encouraging visitors to commit as opposed to having to pay a fee to acquire the same skill elsewhere.

Free training is also a way to address any fears or reservations the visitor may have after viewing the site which the email is attempting to introduce.

If the elements featured are of a rather foreign content or nature to the visitor, then the apprehension towards committing may cause them to be unwilling but if there was a clear indication that some training would be provided for free, this initial apprehension can be positively addressed.

Any free training provided will always be able to act as a positive incentive, because for the visitor, it would ensure that he or she is better equipped to sell or introduce the product or service to others in a professional and knowledgeable manner.

The free training incentive provided can also help to portray the company's commitment levels to the potential prospect.

The willingness to provide such assistance clearly shows the lengths the company is willing to extend in the quest to provide as much assistance as possible to potential prospects. This can be a powerful tool to use to build a future loyal relationship.

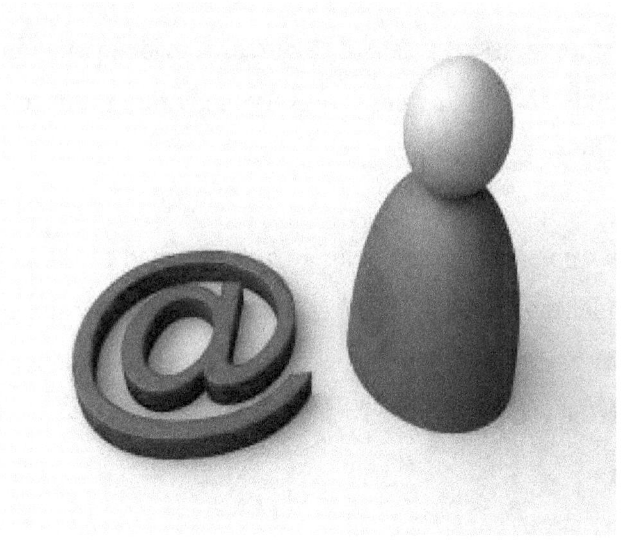

Chapter 8:

Be Tuned Into Your Subscribers Needs

Synopsis

Understanding the subscriber's needs is the only way to successfully make the relevant and suitable matches to ensure resources are not wasted or misused.

The most unnecessary waste of resources is evident when information is randomly sent to anyone and everyone without any consideration or direction.

There is some level of compelling truth attached to the fact that one should identify the important results of what the prospect is looking for or interested in before even considering the particular individual as a suitable prospect.

Keep Them Returning

Being in tune with what people want to achieve, the ways that they would most likely be interested to achieve something and the desired outcomes all make up the information that should be considered early on when designing the email content.

Through the quest of wanting to be tuned into the subscriber's needs focusing some attention on the market areas that seems to lack relevant comprehensive and assisting information could help to provide some idea of why there is a need and how it should be addressed.

When this is adequately identified then steps can be taken to provide the information which would then clearly show the company's ability to be in tune with its subscriber's needs.

When subscribers are assured that their needs are being considered and are of the highest priority, the sense of loyalty that is formed is quite unmatched and definitely worth cultivating. This loyalty element can and usually does play a vital role in retaining the individual as a customer.

Wrapping Up

There are many tools available to help individuals make a success of any business endeavor. However none will be very helpful if one is unable to specifically identify probable needs the customer may have.

If these needs are not addressed and capitalized upon, then there are very little positive results that are going to be forthcoming. Hope fully this book has given you a good head start.

www.ingramcontent.com/pod-product-compliance
Lightning Source LLC
LaVergne TN
LVHW050305200726
843509LV00015B/3167